Walking with the Women of the New Testament
Study Guide
(Volume 2)

Written by Heather Farrell
Designed by Heidi Hillman

For more study helps visit womeninthescriptures.com

How to Use this Study Guide

I am thrilled that you have picked up this study guide, as it means that you are intending to undertake your own personal study of the women of the New Testament. I can testify that this is a journey that will change your heart and possibly your life. I know that as I have studied the women of the New Testament not only have I gained a greater understanding of myself, and my role as a woman in God's Kingdom, but I have also come to better understand Jesus and who he was.

This is a journey that I would love to assist in making a very special and meaningful one for you. Ideally this study guide is to be used in conjunction with my book, *"Walking with the Women of the New Testament"*, but of course you are free to use it in whatever way suits you. I should also specify that I use the King James Version of the Bible and that all my scripture references are taken from that translation. I also assume that you are using the version of the scriptures published by The Church of Jesus Christ of Latter-day Saints. If you are not you can find the Topical Guide and Bible Dictionary I often refer to in this Study Guide here https://www.lds.org/scriptures/study-helps.

With that said, let's get going!

Step 1 -- Print off and organize your Study Guide

If you have the professionally bound copy of this Study Guide then you are ready to go, but if you have the PDF version of this Study Guide you will want to first print it off and then either have it spiral bound or three-hole-punch it and put it in a binder. Either way is fine. The benefit of a binder is that it makes it easy to add in additional pages to each women's study section. On the other hand, the benefit of having it bound is that you won't have to worry about pages getting lost or torn out.

As you go through this study guide you will see study prompts that ask you to use the additional pages found in the back of your study guide-- like the character study, timeline, etc. To use these pages simply photocopy the page from the back of the book and then paste or tape the page into the woman's section you are studying. That way you keep all of your study materials and thoughts about each women organized and easy to find for future reference. It might be helpful to make some photocopies of the additional study pages before you begin your study so you will have them ready for easy access when you need them. Feel free to add in talks, quotes, images or any other study helps you find that enrich your study of the New Testament. Also, you will want to print off the bookmark that is included in the back of the study guide which you will want to photocopy onto cardstock and use it as you go through your study.

Don't worry about getting through the New Testament quickly. Going slowly and really studying these women's lives in depth will be so much more meaningful to you than seeing how quickly you can progress through the books. It might take you three months to complete this study guide, or three years, but either way it will be an incredible journey… so don't rush it.

Step 2--Open up your New Testament and start reading in Matthew.

I have listed the women in the Study Guide as they appear in the New Testament. I only included REAL women, who lived and breathed during the time of the New Testament. This means that you won't find the women in parables, Jesus's teachings or women from the Old Testament (with the exception of the women in Christ's lineage) in this Study Guide. I have left a blank study template in the back of the Study Guide that you can photocopy and add in other women you want to study.

Step 3-- Stop when you find a woman in your reading and take time to understand her story.

I have included a bookmark with this study guide that has questions you can ask yourself each time you come across a new woman. Take the time to think about these questions and record your thoughts in the study guide page dedicated to her. If you need help with this process, or would like to go more in-depth I have included questions and study suggestions in the Study Guide for each woman (or set of women) that will help you dig deeper into their stories and help you find personal application.

At the end of your study guide you will also find additional study pages that will assist you with your study. These pages include:

Character sketch

Use this page to study a character from the scriptures more in-depth. Write their name (or a draw a picture) in the center square and then make a list or a "cloud" of all the attributes, virtues and character traits you see in them as you study. This page can also be used to do a topical study on a word, like "virtue" or "compassion".

Timeline

Use this page to create timelines of events in the New Testament. Don't be too concerned with getting dates right, you just want to get an idea of what order the events happened. Using the "Harmony of the Gospels" or the Bible Chronology in the Bible Dictionary of the LDS Version of the Scriptures may also be helpful.

Storyboard

Use this page to draw (or write) out a story from the New Testament. This can be a visual way to keep track of people, places and events.

Compare and Contrast

There are three different compare and contrast sheets. Choose which one to use depending on how many different accounts there are of the story in the New Testament. For example, you'd want to use the one with four spaces for the story of the Damsel and Maid at the Door because it is told in all four Gospels., but you'd want to use the one with three for the story of the Daughter of Jarius because it is only told in three of the Gospels.

Maps

I have included blank maps of the New Testament Bible lands for you to mark and fill in. Using maps can be a very valuable tool in increasing your understanding of the history and people of the

New Testament. Use the Bible Maps in the the appendix of your LDS version of the Bible (or see them here https://www.lds.org/scriptures/bible-maps) to help you fill them in.

Step 4- Open Up *"Walking With the Women of the New Testament"*

After you have spent time studying the woman for yourself and formed your own ideas about her, then I hope you'd open up my book, *"Walking with the Women of the New Testament"* and read what I have to say about her. You may also find some of my thoughts on my blog, Women in the Scriptures (http://www.womeninthescriptures.com) Don't worry if what I say and what you say don't match up. The beauty of studying the scriptures is that the stories can be interpreted in many different ways—there is no wrong and there is no right way to look at it. Let the Holy Ghost teach you and lead your study and you will learn what YOU need to know. Enjoy what others have to say and their insights, but trust yourself and what the Holy Ghost teaches you.

Step 5-- Share what you have learned about the women of the New Testament with someone else.

I promise that as you delve into your scriptures looking for the women you will find a treasure trove of wisdom and will gain powerful personal revelation. Don't hesitate to share this with others. Trust me the world needs more people sharing the amazing stories of the women in the scriptures. So open your mouth and bear your testimony about what you have learned.

That's it!

You are ready to begin your walk with the women of the New Testament, but before you begin let me leave you with one final thought. In a wonderful talk Elder Dallin H. Oaks gave in January of 1995, entitled "Scripture Reading and Revelation" he said:

"The word of the Lord in the scriptures is like a lamp to guide our feet (seePs. 119:105), and revelation is like a mighty force that increases the lamp's illumination manyfold…Just as continuing revelation enlarges and illuminates the scriptures, so also a study of the scriptures enables men and women to receive revelations. Elder Bruce R. McConkie said, "I sometimes think that one of the best-kept secrets of the kingdom is that the scriptures open the door to the receipt of revelation" . This happens because scripture reading puts us in tune with the Spirit of the Lord." … We do not overstate the point when we say that the scriptures can be a Urim and Thummim to assist each of us to receive personal revelation."

I know what Elder Oaks said is true. The scriptures are the gateway to revelation, and if we want a deeper understanding of our purpose here on the earth, direction in our lives, answers to hard questions and solutions to problems we will find those answers as we commune with the Lord through scripture study.

I hope that as you undertake this journey with the women of the New Testament that you will learn more about your divine mission on this earth. I hope that you will feel of God's incredible love for all of His daughters and feel of His love of you. Most of all, I hope that you will come to better know Jesus Christ and let him change your heart and your life.

Additional Resources to Use in your Study

You will notice as you progress through this Study Guide that in the "Ideas for Additional Study" I will often refer you to other sources. These sources aren't necessary, the Holy Ghost can teach you most everything you need to know, but they can be very useful for better understanding the history, language and people of the New Testament.

1826 Webster's Dictionary

This is one of the oldest English dictionaries and is now available online, as an iPad App, and in printed book form. This dictionary is a valuable resource in your study, especially if you are using the King James version of the Bible. The meaning and usage of many words has changed over the last hundred years, and sometimes our understanding of scriptural passages can be hindered because we are giving a modern meaning to a word whose older meaning is quite different. The 1826 Webster's Dictionary can be found online at http://1828.mshaffer.com/

Strong's Concordance

Strong's Concordance was first published 1890 and is basically an index to the Bible. It allows readers to find the original Hebrew or Greek words that are used in the Bible and to compare how the same word is used in other places in the Bible. It isn't a translation of the Bible but is meant to be used by people who don't read Hebrew or Greek in order to help them gain a more accurate understanding of the Bible.

Strong's Concordance was originally printed in book form and you can still buy and use it that way. They also have concordances that are online and which I have found are much faster and easier to use. My favorite concordance is one I found at a website called Bible Study Tools (http://www.biblestudytools.com/). I have the website saved to my ipad and when I study my scriptures I often pull up the website to check the original meaning of words that seem confusing or out of place to me. The concordance is really a wonderful tool if you want to delve deeper into your scriptures.

If you would like more instructions on how to use one I have a post on my blog, Women in the Scriptures, that explains how to use an online version (http://www.womeninthescriptures.com/2013/07/how-to-use-strongs-concordance-to.html). If you have access to a paper concordance the process is pretty much the same, just more page flipping.

Look at a Different Translation

Sometimes it can be helpful to look at a different translation of the Bible to understand the meaning of a passage. Not only does this sometimes help clarify the language of a passage but I also shows you other ways in which the same words can be translated, giving you a deeper understanding of the passage. If you normally use the King James Version of the Bible you may want to refer to a newer translation and if you normally use a new translation you might want to refer to the King James . It is amazing how looking at the same words from a different perspective can help illuminate their meaning. Personally I like to use a website called Bible Study tools (http://www.biblestudytools.com/) because under "Bible Study" they have a tool called "Compare Translations". This tool allows you to type in any verse in the Bible and see several different translations of the same verse.

Use the Online Scriptures

The Church of Jesus Christ of Latter-day Saints has a wonderful online search tool for the scriptures. It can be found at https://www.lds.org/scriptures. Several times in this Study Guide I will encourage you to look up words or phrases on this website using the "search" bar on the right hand side. The online scriptures can be a fast and easy way to find other ways in which a word, or similar phrase, is used elsewhere in the scriptures. It can also help you connect scriptures together in ways that you might not have thought of before. It can also just be a fast way to find a scripture that you can't remember the reference for!

The COMPLETE Joseph Smith Translation of the Bible

If you are using the LDS version of the Bible you will notice that often throughout the bible there will be footnotes with the abbreviation "JST". This refers to the "Joseph Smith Translation" and indicates that they are passages where Joseph Smith was instructed by God to clarify the meaning of the scriptures. These JST footnotes are extremely helpful in understanding the meaning of certain passages and give much needed insight. Sometimes you will see a footnote that refers you to the Appendix of the Bible where longer translations are included.

It is also important to note that not ALL of the corrections that Joseph Smith made to the Bible are included in the footnotes or the appendix of the LDS Scriptures. To see a COMPLETE listing of all of Joseph Smith's translations you must look at the full Joseph Smith Translation of the Bible (also called Joseph Smith's Inspired Translation of the Bible) which has been published by the Community of Christ. This translation has been available for many years but it has only been in the last decade that the Community of Christ allowed LDS scholars to view the original manuscripts. They found that the versions of Joseph Smith's Inspired Translation of the Bible, which had already been published by the Community of Christ, were true to Joseph Smith's original corrections. There is now a version of the full Joseph Smith Translation of the Bible compiled by BYU scholars and published by Deseret Book that allows you to view the original manuscript and make a side-by-side comparison of it to the KJV (it can be found at http://www.amazon.com/Complete-Joseph-Smith-Translation-Testament/dp/1590384393)

Maps

In the Appendix of the LDS version of the Bible there are several wonderful maps of the New Testament Bible lands. These maps are a wonderful resource and I'd encourage you to look up places that you read about as you study. It is amazing how understanding the geography and location of a woman's story can illuminate and clarify her experience. Using the maps can also help you make connections between other people and events.

Women Gathered in Prayer with the Apostles

Scripture References:

Acts 1:14

Words I looked up:

What I know about them:

Questions I have about them:

My thoughts on the Women Gathered in Prayer with the Apostles:

Additional scriptures I studied:

Ideas for additional study:

- What events occurred before this meeting? What events occurred after?

- List who was included in this meeting? Why do you think these individual were present?

- Use the search option in the online scriptures to search for the phrase "with one accord". What other times are people gathered to pray "with one accord". What do you think this phrase means?

- Why might it be significant that women were included in this meeting?

- What does it teach you about the way in which the early Christian church operated after Jesus' death?

Sapphira

Scripture References:

Acts 5:1-11

Words I looked up:

What I know about her:

Questions I have about her:

My thoughts about Sapphira:

Additional scriptures I studied:

Ideas for additional study:

• Do a character sketch of Sapphira. What can you learn from her? How might you use her story in a talk or lesson to illustrate a principle?

• Study Acts 4. What type of experiences had the saints experienced previous to Sapphira's story? What type of covenants had they made?

• Study "Covenant" in the Bible Dictionary (page 651). What can her story teach you about making and keeping covenants?

• Why do you think that her consequence of her lie was so swift and immediate? How did the people react after they heard her story?

• Is it ever okay to lie? Why or why not?

• Think about the last week. Were you always COMPLETELY honest? What did you do well? What could you improve on?

• What is your example teaching the youth and children in your life? How are you helping them to learn to keep covenants.

Widows who were Neglected

Scripture References:

Acts 6:1

Words I looked up:

What I know about them:

Questions I have about them:

My thoughts about the
Widows who were Neglected:

Additional scriptures I studied:

Ideas for additional study:

• What two groups are highlighted in this story? What would they have had in common? How would they have been different?

• Use the footnotes to look up what the "daily ministration" was. How might these widows have been left out of it? Why?

• Have you ever had an experience when you felt that you or someone else was being treated unfairly in the church? How did you react? How was it similar to these saints? How was it different?

• How did the 12 apostles respond to the people's concerns? What new church position did they create and who did they call to it? (see Acts 6: 3-6). What might be the equivalent of the position these men filled in the church today?

• What can this story teach you about how to handle inequality in the church?

• How might this story be useful to a Ward council or others in church leadership positions?

Samaritan Women baptized by Philip

Scripture References:

Acts 8:12

Words I looked up:

What I know about them:

Questions I have about them:

My thoughts about the Samaritan Women
baptized by Philip:

Additional scriptures I studied:

Ideas for additional study:

• Who was Philip? See "Philip" (entry #2) in the Bible Dictionary. Use the scripture references listed to study what stories he included in? What type of man was he?

• How does this story and the story of the Samaritan Woman at the Well (see John 4) relate? What prophesy did Jesus make to her that is fulfilled in this story?

• Think about the missionary experiences you have had in your life. When have you planted seeds? When have you watered seeds? When have you harvested? Take time to record some of your missionary experiences in your journal.

• In Acts 8 Philip had several significant missionary experiences. Study the chapter and list which groups of people he shares the gospel with. What does this teach you about how the early Christian church was expanding? What can it teach you about God's love for His children?

• If you are not familiar with Samaritans and their beliefs and role in the New Testament culture take the time to study them in the Bible Dictionary (see page 768).

Candace, queen of the Ethiopians

Scripture References:

Acts 8:27

Words I looked up:

What I know about her:

Questions I have about her:

My thoughts about Candace,
queen of the Ethiopians:

Additional scriptures I studied:

Ideas for additional study:

• For a better understanding of what the title "Candace" means and who this woman was see "Candace" on page 167 in *"Walking with the Women in the New Testament"*.

• Look up the word "Eunuch" in the Bible Dictionary. It might be interesting to read the other references listed as well, especially Christ's teachings about eunuchs in Matthew 19:12. How might these men's experiences be applicable today?

• How might this eunuch have been instrumental in spreading Christianity in Ethiopia?

• Look up "Ethiopia" in the Bible Dictionary and study the additional references. What other significant people in the Bible came from this area of the world?

• Ethiopia was also known as "Cush" and looking up that reference in the Bible Dictionary will give you even more insight into this area of the world and its history. It is also important to note that this area is not visible on any of the maps in the LDS Edition of the Bible. It might be helpful to get online and find one so that you understand where it is.

• What impresses you about this story? How might you use it in a talk or in a lesson? What principle could you teach from it?

Tabitha

Scripture References:

Acts 9:36-42

Words I looked up:

What I know about her:

Questions I have about her:

My thoughts about Tabitha:

Additional scriptures I studied:

Ideas for additional study:

• Identify Joppa on a Bible map. Identify Lydda on a Bible map.

• Does Tabitha remind you of any woman that you know? Who? Why?

• What is her Greek name? What is her Hebrew name? Why might she be known by both of these names?

• What happened previous to Tabitha's story? What happens in the chapter after her story? Why do you think her story is told in between these events?

• How might her story have been influential in the spreading of Christianity?

• Why do you think Peter was called when she died? What does his quick response to the news of her death tell you about his relationship to her?

• How can you relate to Tabitha? What miraculous events have you experienced in your life?

Mary, the Mother of John Mark

Scripture References:

Acts 12:12
Col 4:10

Words I looked up:

What I know about her:

Questions I have about her:

My thoughts about Mary, the Mother of John Mark:

Additional scriptures I studied:

Ideas for additional study:

• What was the religious climate like in Jerusalem at the time of her story? What risks did she and the other Christians face?

• Why do you think Peter came to her house after his release from prison? What does that tell you about the importance of her home to the early saints?

• Study the life of her son Mark by looking up "Mark" in the Bible Dictionary and studying the references listed. What can you learn about her through her son?

• She was also the sister of Barnabas, who was one of Paul's missionary companions (see Colossians 4:10). Look up "Barnabas" in the Bible Dictionary and study the references listed for him. What can you learn about her from her brother's life? What experiences would she have had in common with him?

Rhoda

Scripture References:

Acts 12:13-15

Words I looked up:

What I know about her:

Questions I have about her:

My thoughts about Rhoda:

Additional scriptures I studied:

Ideas for additional study:

• Draw a story board sketch of the events in Acts 12. What role does Rhoda play in the story?

• Create a character sketch for her. What virtues and attributes does she exemplify?

• How might you use her story in a lesson or in a talk? How might the young women in your life benefit from her story?

• How is her story similar/different to that of the women at the empty tomb (see Matthew 28, Mark 16, Luke 24, John 20)?

• Have you ever had an experience where you bore testimony when it was hard to or when you weren't believed? How did that make you feel?

• Study the word "damsel" in the Strongs Concordance. Which word is used for her? What can this tell you about her family and who she was? You might also want to study the word translated as "damsel" in the story of the daughter of Jarius (Mark 5:41). What is different about these two words, what can it tell you about the difference between these two young women?

Devout and Honorable Women of Jews and Greeks

Scripture References:

Acts 13:50
Acts 17: 4, 12

Words I looked up:

What I know about them:

Questions I have about them:

My thoughts on Devout and Honorable
Women of Jews and Greeks:

Additional scriptures I studied:

Ideas for additional study:

• Study the two stories (Acts 13 and 17) and do a compare and contrast. What is similar about Paul's experiences in these two places? What is different about them?

• What type of influence did the women in both of these communities have on the opinions of those around them and how Paul and his companions were treated?

• How have you seen women influence people around them—for good or for bad?

• Look up the words "devout' and "honorable" in the 1828 Webster Dictionary. What do these words mean to you? Can you think of women that you know that you consider "devout" and "honorable"? How do they make their influence felt?

• You may also want to study the talk "The Moral Force of Women" by Elder D. Todd Christofferson (in the November 2013 Ensign). How do these women exemplify what he was teaching?

Eunice and Lois

Scripture References:

2 Tim 1:15
Acts 16:1

Words I looked up:

What I know about them:

Questions I have about them:

My thoughts on Eunice and Lois:

Additional scriptures I studied:

Ideas for additional study:

• What is Eunice's marital situation? What would have been unique about her position? What challenges can you imagine came with it?

• In 2 Timothy 1:5 Paul says that they had "unfeigned faith". Look up the word "unfeigned" in the 1828 Webster Dictionary. How do you imagine that Eunice and Lois demonstrated this type of faith?

•Study the life of Timothy by using the Bible Dictionary (see page 785) to obtain a list of references about him. You might even want to do a character sketch or a timeline for him, documenting the experiences he went through in his life and ministry. What type of man was he? What can his character tell you about Eunice and Lois?

• In Acts 16:3 it tells how Paul circumcised Timothy before he traveled with him, which was an unusual circumstance. The idea that circumcision was no longer needed (because of the atonement of Jesus Christ) was a difficult concept for the Jews to grasp (imagine if all of sudden we didn't have to baptize people any more) and one that is struggled with throughout the New Testament. This is an interesting topic to study and making a list of all the references to "circumcision" in the Topical Guide will give you a good place to begin a study of this topic—especially concentrating on the listings in the New Testament and Book of Mormon.

Lydia

Scripture References:

Acts 16: 11-15, 40

Words I looked up:

What I know about her:

Questions I have about her:

My thoughts on Lydia:

Additional scriptures I studied:

Ideas for additional study:

• Locate Philippi on a map. Locate Thyatira (see verse 14) on a map.

• Read Acts 16: 1-12 and make special note of what experiences Paul had before he came to Philippi.

• What was Lydia's occupation? What blessings would have come from her business? What challenges would have come from it?

• What evidence do you see that Lydia was prepared and seeking truth? How might in D&C 123:32 apply to her? You may want to do a character sketch for her.

• What did Lydia do after hearing Paul's message? How do you welcome the prophet, the missionaries, and the truth into your home?

• Be sure to read all of Acts 16. What other events happened in Philippi? How might Lydia have been involved in these? How would they have affected her?

• How is Lydia similar to the story of prison guard in Acts 16:25-40? How is she different?

Damsel Possessed with a Spirit of Divination

Scripture References:

Acts 16:16-19

Words I looked up:

What I know about her:

Questions I have about her:

My thoughts about the Damsel Possessed with a Spirit of Divination:

Additional scriptures I studied:

Ideas for additional study:

• Where did this damsel live? What other woman/women have you studied that also lived there?

• How old do you imagine her? How does her age affect your understanding of this story?

• Look up "Soothsayer" in the Bible Dictionary and study the other references listed. How is this gift different than the gift of prophesy? You may want to study "Prophecy" in "The Guide to the Scriptures" found in the Study Helps on LDS.org

• Why do you think Paul's heart was "grieved" because of this girl?

• What do you think this girl's life was like after her healing? What do you imagine happened to her?

• How might this story be applicable today?

Damaris

Scripture References:

Acts 17:34

Words I looked up:

What I know about her:

Questions I have about her:

My thoughts about Damaris:

Additional scriptures I studied:

Ideas for additional study:

• Look up "Athens" in the Bible Dictionary. There is also a picture in the map section at the end of the New Testament that can give you a better visual image of where Paul would have been when he was teaching.

• Who else listened to Paul's message? Who believed him?

• What do you think made Damaris different than other Athenians?

• Damaris heard Paul preach about the true nature of God. Understanding the nature of God is the basis for any strong testimony. In the Topical Guide there are 13 pages under the heading of "God" which deal with every aspect of God's nature. Choose two or three of the aspects of God you would better like to understand and study the references listed. You may also want to write down some specific questions you have and ponder them while you study.

Priscilla

Scripture References:

Acts 18:2-3, 18-20, 24-26

Rom. 16: 3-5

1 Cor. 16:19

2 Tim 4:19

Words I looked up:

What I know about her:

Questions I have about her:

My thoughts on Priscilla:

Additional scriptures I studied:

Ideas for additional study:

• Do a character sketch for Priscilla. What do you find striking about her?

• What was her occupation? What do you imagine this type of work would have been like?

• What places did Priscilla live? Locate them on the maps in the appendix and then mark them on your own map. You might even want to draw a timeline of her life.

• Write a list of everyone that Priscilla would have known. How do you imagine she influenced them? What services and sacrifices did she give for the church?

• What did Paul think of Priscilla? What evidence do you see that she was an important figure in the early church?

• What can you learn from the relationship between Aquilla and Priscilla? What can they teach us about equality in marriage?

• What can she teach you about missionary work? What do you need to do to become the type of missionary she was?

Wives and Children of Tyre

Scripture References:

Acts 21:4-6

What I know about them:

Words I looked up:

Questions I have about them:

My thoughts on the Wives and Children of Tyre:

Additional scriptures I studied:

Ideas for additional study:

• Locate Tyre on the map (located in the appendix of the Bible) entitled "The Missionary Journeys of the Apostle Paul". This story occurs on his third journey. Locate where he went before and after this story. Also for a very in-depth scripture study you could use the blank map in the back of the study guide and re-draw all of Paul's missionary journeys, making special note of the places where he would have encountered different women.

• What did the people of Tyre tell Paul? How did they know this?

• Imagine this scene in your mind? How would you have felt if you were one of these women saying goodbye to Paul? What would you have said in your prayer?

• In verse 3 the ship Paul travels on is called "her". Why do you think that things like ships and airplanes are often given female names?

• Make sure to read all of Acts 21. What happens to Paul after he leaves Tyre? Do you think he made the right choice? Why or why not?

Four Daughters of Philip

Scripture References:

Acts 21:9

Words I looked up:

What I know about them:

Questions I have about them:

My thoughts about the Four
Daughters of Philip:

Additional scriptures I studied:

Ideas for additional study:

• Where did these young women live?

• Look up their father Philip in the Bible Dictionary (see page 750). What other stories that you have studied was he in? What was his role in the church?

• Look up the word "evangelist" in the Bible Dictionary (see page 668).

• What gift of the spirit did these young women possess? Study about gifts of the spirit in D&C 46 (also Moroni 10: 8- 24 and 1 Corinthians 12: 1-11). Which spiritual gifts do you have and how are you developing and using them?

• How can you encourage the young women in your life to develop their spiritual gifts?

• How are these young women similar to the women called "prophetesses" in the Bible (see Judges 4:4, Exodus 15:20; 2 Chronicles 34:32 and Luke 2:36)?

Paul's Sister

Scripture References:

Acts 23:16

Words I looked up:

What I know about her:

Questions I have about her:

My thoughts about Paul's sister:

Additional scriptures I studied:

Ideas for additional study:

• Draw a storyboard of the events that take place in Acts 23. Who are the main characters and what part do they each play? How does Paul's family influence the outcome of the story?

• Study the differences between a Pharisee and Sadducee by looking up those words in the Bible Dictionary. The chart on page 211 of "Walking with the Women of the New Testament" is an excellent resource.

• We don't know much about this woman, but what can you surmise about her from the way in which her son treats and interacts with Paul and with the other Jews?

• Put yourself in her shoes for a moment and imagine that your brother was Paul. What would your feelings be?

Bernice and Drusilla

Scripture References:

Acts 24:24
Acts 25:13-14, 23
Acts 26:30

What I know about them:

Words I looked up:

Questions I have about them:

My thoughts on Bernice and Drusilla:

Additional scriptures I studied:

Ideas for additional study:

• These women are both well documented historical figures. To understand their family history and lives better make sure to read their story on page 213 of "Walking with the Women of the New Testament". The Herodian Family Tree chart on page 217 should also be helpful.

• What is similar about these two women's stories? What is different? How much time passed in between their two encounters with Paul?

• How might Bernice and Drusilla have changed from simply "hearers of the word" to be truly converted? What would they have needed to have done?

• How can you relate to them? Have you ever felt prompted to change something in your life but have hesitated because it seemed too hard or too scary?

• Are you truly converted to gospel of Jesus Christ? How can you know when someone is converted?

Women of Romans 16

Scripture References:

Romans 16:1-15

What I know about them:

Words I looked up:

Questions I have about them:

My thoughts on the Women of Romans 16:

Additional scriptures I studied:

Ideas for additional study:

• It can be tricky to identify all the women in this chapter. Use the chart on page 226 of *"Walking with the Women in the New Testament"* to help you fill in the chart in your study journal. It might also help to mark the women in the verses so you can indentify them easily in the future.

• Once you have identified all the women read through each woman's listing and write down everything you can learn about her. Even though the individual verses are brief by looking at the group as a whole you can learn much about who they were and how they interacted.

• Once you have a list of women you might also want to make a separate list with all the men's names and what influence they might have had on the women.

• Use the Bible Dictionary and look up "Pauline Epistles" and read the listing under "Epistles to the Romans".

• What do these women all have in common? What impresses you about them?

• What different "titles" does Paul give many of these women? What type of work do you think these women were engaged in?

Scripture References:

1 Corinthians 1:11

What I know about her:

Words I looked up:

Questions I have about her:

My thoughts about Chloe:

Additional scriptures I studied:

Ideas for additional study:

• Identify Corinth on a map. Look up "Corinth" in the Bible Dictionary. You may also want to read the listing of 1 Corinthians in the "Pauline Epistles" section of the Bible Dictionary for some historical background.

• Paul's 1st epistle to the Corinthians deals with many of the contentions that had been brought to his attention. Read through the whole epistle (yes, all 15 chapters) slowly and make a list of all the contentions, problems, and questions that Paul addressed. It may be helpful to use the compare and contrast pages in the back and make a column for each chapter, putting bullet points for the main ideas discussed in that chapter. When you are finished look at the book as a whole--- what trends and connections do you see?

• There are many confusing things about women taught in the epistle. Make sure you write down your questions and the passages that are especially confusing to you. Slow down on those ones and let the Holy Ghost guide you to where to find the answers you need.

• Chapter 7 deals with marriage. Be sure to read the chapter heading for that chapter as it has important clarifying information. Also, be sure to study the JST translation in the Appendix for 1 Corinthians 7:29-33. Understanding the context is KEY to understanding what Paul was teaching in 1 Corinthians.

Euodia and Syntyche

Scripture References:

Phillip 4: 2-3

Words I looked up:

What I know about them:

Questions I have about them:

My thoughts about Euodia and Syntyche:

Additional scriptures I studied:

Ideas for additional study:

• The name given in the KJV is Euodias, which is a male name and so it is possible that this story is about a disagreement between a man and a woman. On the other hand many scholars feel that a better translation of the name would be Euodia, which is a female name. Either might be correct. How does this story's meaning change if it involves a man and woman or if it is two women?

• What does it mean to have your name "written in the book of life" ? Study the references listed in the Topical Guide under "Book of Life." What does it tell you about these women that their names were "written in the book of life"?

• What other women that you have studied lived in Philippi?

• To understand the context of the book of Philippians it may help to study the listing "Philippi" in the Bible Dictionary or look up "Pauline Epistles" and read the listing under "Epistles to the Philippians".

• What does Paul suggest that the Philippians do to increase their unity? How might you apply this principle in your life?

Claudia

Scripture References:

2 Timothy 4:21

Words I looked up:

What I know about her:

Questions I have about her:

My thoughts about Claudia:

Additional scriptures I studied:

Ideas for additional study:

• To understand the historical context of 2 Timothy look up "Pauline Epistles" in the Bible Dictionary. 2 Timothy is listed under the "Fourth Group" of epistles. Study ing this reference will give you a better understanding of the situation Paul was in when he wrote to Timothy.

• Where was she living? Who else did Paul list with Claudia and why did he include their names?

• We don't know much about her but what can you glean from Paul's letter? What intimate details can you pick out? What do you imagine her role was in Paul's life at this point? Do you think that she suspected that Paul would soon be killed?

• What challenges would she have faced? What was some of the last council that Paul gave before his death?

Apphia

Scripture References:

Philemon 1:2

Words I looked up:

What I know about her:

Questions I have about her:

My thoughts about Apphia:

Additional scriptures I studied:

Ideas for additional study:

• Study a list of those who held churches in their homes (see "Apphia" on page 251 of "*Walking With the Women of the New Testament*") . How many of them were women? What impresses you about the people in this list?

• Think about the Church building you currently attend. Write a list about all the different ways in which that building is used throughout the year. What activities would be the same as those that early Christians may have participated in? What would have been challenging about having the church hosted in your home.

• Have you ever lived somewhere where were the church was hosted in a home? If so make sure you have written about it in your personal journal. If not, it might be interesting to talk to someone who has and learn about their experiences and how they might have been similar/different to New Testament women.

• Look up "Philemon" in the Bible Dictionary. You could also look up "Pauline Epis tles" in the Bible Dictionary and read the entry "epistle to Philemon" on page 746. After reading this brief history go back and study the epistle again. What additional insights did you gain?

The Elect Lady

Scripture References:

2 John

Words I looked up:

What I know about her:

Questions I have about her:

My thoughts about The Elect Lady:

Additional scriptures I studied:

Ideas for additional study:

• Who wrote this epistle? You might want to study "John, Epistles of" in the Bible Dictionary.

• Using the online scriptures type in the word "elect" and study the references it pulls up. What do you notice about how this word is used? What might it tell you about this woman?

• You might also want to study the word "elect" and "lady" in the Strongs Concor dance. What do these words tell you about who she was and what her role was in the early church?

• Think of all the women in the New Testament that you have studied. Do you think this woman could be one of them? Who?

• Make a list of the main points that John wrote to her about. What is interesting to you about what he wrote?

Scripture References:

What I know about her:

Words I looked up:

Questions I have about her:

Time Line

Compare and Contrast

Compare and Contrast

Compare and Contrast

Character Study

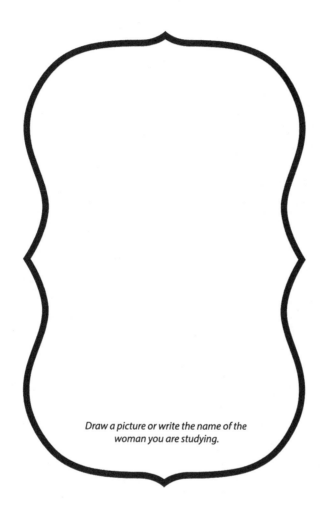

Draw a picture or write the name of the
woman you are studying.

Time Line

Story board for:

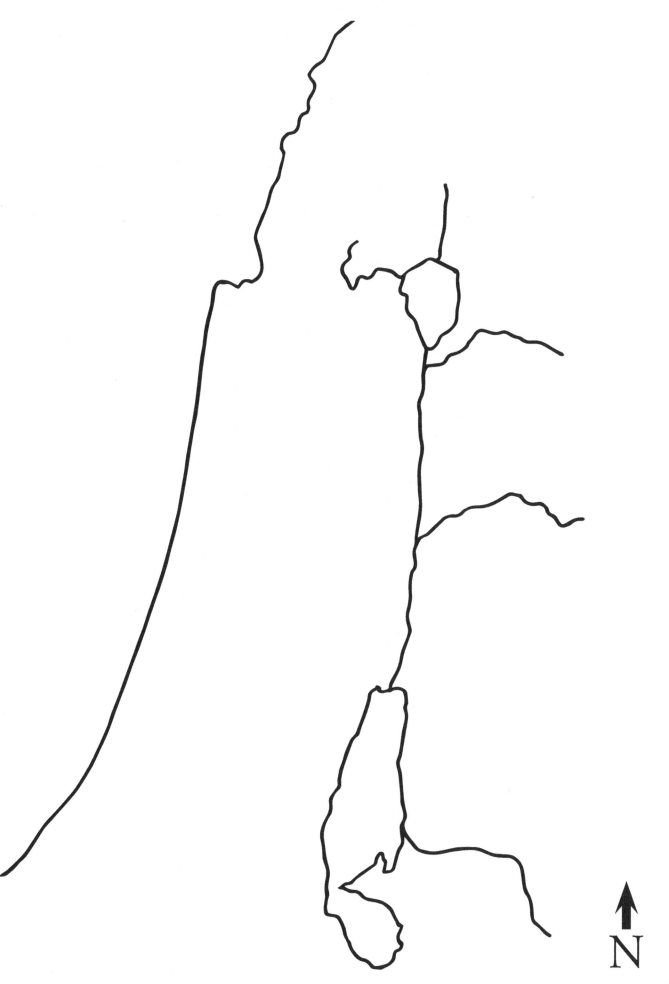

N

N